CRACK THE PROPERTY INVESTMENT CODE!

YOUR ULTIMATE STEP-BY-STEP GUIDELINE TO PROPERTY IN-VESTMENT

FROM PROPERTY INVESTOR MENTOR'S PERSPECTIVE

By Mpho Hadebe

Copyright © 2020 by Ellion Property Solutions Pty LTD

Published by Ellion Property Solutions Pty LTD

License Notes

All rights reserved. This book or any portion thereof may not be reproduced, stored in retrieval system, or transmitted, in any manner whatsoever, electronic, mechanical, photocopy, recording, without the express written permission of the publisher except for the use of brief quotations in a book review.

Disclaimer

This book is designed to provide guideline information that the author believes to be accurate on the subject matter it covers. However, it is understandable that neither the author nor the publisher is offering individualized advice tailored to any specific portfolio or any individual's particular needs. Also, it doesn't render investment advice or other professional services, such as legal or accounting advice. A competent professional's services should be sought if one needs expert assistance in areas that include investment, legal, and accounting advice.

This publication references data of experience collected over some time through sources, including publications and research that have been proven reliable but cannot be guaranteed insofar as they may or may not apply to any particular person's financial or tax situation. A specific individual's experience does not guarantee future performance. Past results, in addition to an individual's country laws and regulations, change over time, which could change the status of the information in this guideline. This guideline is intended to serve as the basis for any property investment decision as a recommendation to any specific property investor.

No warranty is made concerning the accuracy or completeness of the information contained herein, and both the author and the publisher specifically disclaim any responsibility for any reliability, loss, or risk, personal or otherwise, which is incurred as a consequence, directly or indirectly, of the use and application of the content of this guideline.

Table of Contents

DISCLAIMER II

PREFACE V

ACKNOWLEDGEMENT VI

INTRODUCTION: MY JOURNEY 1

CHAPTER 1: WHY YOU SHOULD INVEST IN PROPERTY 8

CHAPTER 2: SKILLS DEVELOPMENT 10

CHAPTER 3: THE POWER OF HAVING A MENTOR 11

CHAPTER 4: ROLES AND RESPONSIBILITIES OF A MENTOR AND MENTEE 13

CHAPTER 5: SETTING OUT GOALS 15

CHAPTER 6: EXIT STRATEGIES 18

CHAPTER 7: COMPARATIVE MARKET ANALYSIS 20

CHAPTER 8: BUSINESS PARTNERSHIP 22

CHAPTER 9: BUSINESS OPERATING STRUCTURE 23

CHAPTER 10: PROPERTY INVESTMENT PROFESSIONAL TEAM 24

CHAPTER 11: PROPERTY BUYING PROCESS FLOW 26

CHAPTER 12: PROPERTY SELLING PROCESS FLOW 28

CHAPTER 13: PROPERTY VIEWING 30

CHAPTER 14: PROPERTY FINANCING 33

CHAPTER 15: SOURCING OF DISTRESSED PROPERTIES .. 35

CHAPTER 16: BUYING FROM PRIVATE AUCTION 36

CHAPTER 17: BUYING FROM THE SHERIFF'S AUCTION .. 40

CHAPTER 18: FORECLOSURE 42

CHAPTER 19: REFINANCING 45

CHAPTER 20: HOUSE FLIPPING (CAPITAL FLIP) 46

CHAPTER 21: BUY-TO-LET 49

CHAPTER 22: MULTI-LET STRATEGY 53

CHAPTER 23: SELLER FINANCING STRATEGY (INSTALLMENT SALE) 54

CHAPTER 24: LAND SUBDIVISION 56

CHAPTER 25: LAND CONSOLIDATION 58

CHAPTER 26: RENT-TO-OWN 59

CHAPTER 27: RENT-TO-RENT 60

CLOSING 61

ABOUT THE AUTHOR 63

Preface

This guideline has been designed with a sole purpose of creating a strong foundation for property investors to invest creatively in the residential property business in order to understand the fundamental processes thereof, based on the property investor's mentor perspective. It covers various aspects of acquiring the necessary tools and knowledge that are critical when investing in residential property from a strategic point of view and that is based on the *South African property markets and system.*

The book covers subjects that include, but not limited to why you should invest in the property business as one of the lucrative income streams, and the required skills to be a creative property investor. It also emphasizes the importance of working with a specialized property investor, mentor, or coach. The reader will also learn how to set up their property investment goals as well as strategies that the reader will have to implement to achieve those goals.

This guideline illustrates the most important and critical process flows, which are involved in buying distressed properties, buying from distressed owners or sellers below property market value, and selling or letting property at the market value. You will also learn how to identify and acquire these properties.

The strategies covered in this guideline include but not limited to: foreclosure, refinancing, house flipping, buy-to-let, multi-lets, seller financing (installment strategy), rent-to-rent strategy, rent-to-buy strategy, and more. This guide will work as your property investor mentor in your pocket and help you to crack the code of investing in residential property.

Acknowledgement

I would like to acknowledge the following amazing and inspirational people for their support and contribution towards making this book come to life:

First and foremost, I would like to thank Zonke Mbatha, my life partner, and pillar of strength. She played an important role in proofreading and editing this book. She supported me through difficult times. When I wanted to give up, she used to encourage, motivate, and help me to realize my full potential towards becoming an entrepreneur, which I aspired to be. I thank you from the bottom of my heart.

Special thanks to my family, starting with my mother, Rebecca Buthelezi. Her love, understanding, and support uplifted me during difficult times; she always encouraged, prayed for me. My big brother Rufus, your role was as an indirect mentor, and you've always supported me morally and financially. My sister Serite was able to send my kids and me some money occasionally so that they could go to school out of her minimum wage. My son Tebogo and my twins, Siphe and Sihle, as young as you were, you showed me love, support, and respect despite all the odds.

My friends, Mthobisi Sibisi (Mtho), Smiso Dlamini, and Sibusiso (Gwajo) Shabalala — you were the best friends anyone could ask for. You always listened to my ideas and encouraged me to continue and pursue them even during difficult times

Introduction: My Journey

Why do you invest in any business before acquiring necessary knowledge and skill to manage it?

Most people want to invest in property but do not know where to start. Some have attended seminars and read books but are still in the dark. Some have already started, but the results are not as great as they anticipated. Needless to say, now they are wondering why. Unfortunately, there is no one-size-fits-all answer to this question. However, it all depends on one's desires, goals, knowledge, strategies, willingness to learn, willingness to change, and sacrifices that a person is willing to make to be where he or she wants to be. Nonetheless, if you are one of the people mentioned above, this book is for you, and it intends to guide and show you some critical steps you will need to follow when you are investing, particularly in the residential property business.

Never say never! I used to say I would never become an entrepreneur, let alone become a professional property investor, or even be willing and able to write this offering. This was because I had no proper financial education, knowledge, and I thought I was comfortable with my monthly salary. I had a house and a beautiful luxury German car... all in all, I told myself that my life was well balanced as I could satisfy most of my needs.

Moreover, I thought I had learned enough as I had good experience and qualifications, which included but not limited to the following: Btech in Civil Engineering, Master's Degree in Shipping and Transport (Economics and Supply Chain) from Netherland, Certificate in Management Development Program from the University of KwaZulu-Natal, Certificate in Project Management from Nelson Mandela University as well as registered as Professional Engineering Technician with Engineering Council of South Africa (ECSA). This made it easy for me to find any job related to my field of study.

In the year 2015, something special happened to me and changed my life forever. So, I got a job in Durban as Senior Project Manager. Interestingly, in this workplace I met some great colleagues that inspired me to think differently and to be business-minded. As usual, with my colleagues during lunchtime, we used to sit together and discuss the matters and affairs of the company, departmental and other issues that were affecting our lives in general. However, during this one particular day, one of my friends/colleagues spoke and provided a summary of the book called *Rich Dad Poor Dad* by Robert Kiyosaki, and he recommended that we all read it; hence we can change our ways of thinking. The other colleagues recommended that we should also buy and read the following books: *Who Moved My Cheese* by Spencer Johnson and *The Secret* by Rhonda Byrne, but am not going to give the details of these books here but I highly recommend that you read them as well maybe they might change your life too.

I must confess, the conversation we had during that lunchtime changed my life in a manner in which I can't express. Thanks to my ex-colleagues: Muzi Ntuli, Owen Mkhwanazi, and Sfiso Mavuso for opening my mind and eyes. From that day, I didn't waste any time further, but I downloaded the Kindle App (for reading eBooks) and purchased these books from Amazon. From that day on, I read every page of those books, and, as a result, I started developing an interest in pursuing property business. Besides, reading them has led me to discover other books that were more related to real estate investment, which provided more insight as to how to invest in the property business, creatively.

Lesson learned: *Surround yourself with people that contribute positively to your wellbeing, mental capacity and spiritually, so that you can grow and reach new heights of your desired goals.*

Given the fact that I had already started investing in real estate since I had three properties in my portfolio, I bought my first property (bachelor flat) in 2007, after I had relocated from Empangeni to East London. Unfortunately, because I didn't have proper knowledge of investing in real estate, I bought an overpriced property. The question would be, how did I realize that the property was overpriced? After more than 11 years of owning the property, when I placed it on the market for sale, I couldn't sell it for more than eight months. As a consequence, I had to sell it at the price below what I bought it for. Even during rental periods when I rented it out, I had to subsidize it with money out of my pocket as the rental income was not sufficient to make bond monthly payments, insurance, levies, and rates. All in all, with this investment, I lost more than R250 000 during the purchase, renting, and selling of this property.

As my interest in investing in real estate has risen, I was once approached on LinkedIn by one of business plan writers who promised to write a business plan and apply for funding from the government's grant schemes. I accepted the proposal since I had already had in mind some business concepts. Then I was asked to make a payment of R120 000 before they commence with the writing of my business plan. However, I managed to negotiate the fee down from R120 000 to R80 000. To obtain this amount, I had to use my annual bonus and savings so that I could be able to pay for their services. We met and signed the documents, and I made the payment. However, a week after all this paperwork, I phoned to track the progress only to find that no one was answering the phone... I have been scammed, I realized! I decided to drive to their offices in Amanzimtoti only to find that they have relocated to Cape Town, and they can no longer be contacted.

Lesson learned: *Conduct thorough research about any company that you want to work with or use their services and never pay in full for the services to be rendered before they are concluded.*

Despite losing this big amount, which was more than twice my monthly salary, I didn't give up on my dream of becoming a property investor. I continued to read more books on real estate investment, and I also developed the urge to quit my job as I thought it was depriving me of achieving my goals. I registered my company in the year 2016, and it was going to be used for investing in real estate. In the year 2017, during February, Transnet introduced the campaign to which employees could voluntarily take early retirement. To that end, I didn't hesitate to take that opportunity, my application was approved, and I left Transnet in May 2017 with 11 years of work experience.

My decision to take early retirement was taken after consultations with my family. However, I must say that I regret to have taken that decision too early because I wish I knew then that investing in property while you are still working is easy. When you buy using the bank, it only requires your three months' bank statement and pay slip. If your affordability is good, you have a deal, so I wouldn't have resigned. However, at the same time, I am glad that I took that decision, even though I didn't have a proper and sustainable plan as I didn't have a mentor who was going to guide me to achieve my goals.

However, in August 2017, I saw an advert on Facebook to participate in the Free Property Investment Seminar. I attended this seminar, and it taught me a lot and motivated me to continue with my plans for investing in real estate. After that free seminar, there was a follow-up training known as Master Class for Property Investors, which took two days for R7000. When I thought that I have learned everything and was ready to start investing in property, then a mentorship program was introduced, which I also signed up for. It was costly (as I thought with my lack of financial education) since I paid about R35 000. The only challenge I experienced in this mentorship and coaching program was that I didn't receive enough information as to how it would assist me. What happened is that the package that I chose was only suitable for people who possess property investment experience, who needed some little bit of push and assistance from the coach. This package wasn't good for me, and I was further losing interest in the coaching sessions as I was not gaining that inspiration.

Lesson learned: *You must always opt to ask as to which package will be well suitable for you based on your experience and financial capacity. However, for an inexperienced person, it's not possible to know which questions to ask* as you may be excited about what has been introduced to you. That said, it is the duty of the person introducing the product to clearly explain to you as to how that product would be of benefit rather than to chase after the sales and make money.

I eventually deviated from my initial plans (property investment) as I needed something else that could keep me going by receiving monthly cash flow. I bought a tipper truck at a price of R300 000, and it was deployed on a construction site. The unfortunate part is that after the purchase day, when I was driving the truck towards its designated site from Durban to Dundee, the truck broke down (engine failure). It took me more than two months to fix the engine, and it ended up costing me more than R250 000 cash. This amount was never enough because the truck did not finish a week without breakdowns. Thus, it resulted in lots of traveling, buying spare parts, towing fees, and mechanics fees. After eight months, I decided to sell that truck less than the amount I bought it for. Unfortunately, no one was willing to buy it. The truck was unprofitable and out of operation for more than two years. At the same time, I was still liable for its annual registration fee that ended up costing me about R100 000, including penalties.

Lesson learned: *When you start a certain business, focus only on it until you can be satisfied that it is well established, sustainable and can be operational in your absentia. When you start a new business, make sure that you find someone who has been involved in a similar business before so that you may learn from their experience and avoid going through the same pitfall they went through. In short, you must have a mentor.*

During the truck fiasco and property investment mentorship, I bought a vacant land (6000m2) in Nqutu. This property was purchased through private auction at the total cost of R100 000, excluding VAT, estate agent commission fee, and transfer costs. After 8 months of the purchase of this property, I flipped it for R600 000 and I made a profit of approximately R430 000, given the fact that I didn't even put one pole in the ground. I continued to flip more properties following my ten-year investment goals.

Few months down the line, I was approached via LinkedIn by the Co-founder of Wealth Alliance company Think and Grow Rich, located in South Africa. She asked me if I would be available to take a position as Mentor for property investors based in Durban. We discussed the job requirements and salary arrangements, and I agreed to the effect. I went through some training whereby I used to work for no salary. Eventually, I started working officially, but unfortunately, when I sent my payment invoice (as I was working as a consultant) to be processed, I was informed that they made a mistake. The rate I have used is incorrect, and it should be half of what I have claimed. I was shocked by the news and tried to fight back, but it was like pouring water on the back of a duck. With the big picture in mind (learn more, establish network), I didn't quit. I worked there for more than 6 months then resigned to established my company call Ellion Property Solutions.

Lesson learned: *Always strive to have a signed agreement for whatever contract you engage in. Secondly, when you start a new job, don't work for the sake of getting a salary but try to collect information and learn more so that you can be able to stand on your own in the future. Don't reinvent the wheel; copy and improve from the existing systems and differentiate yourself as the best service provider to your clients.*

Enough about myself, let's dive into what you bought this book for! This guide seeks to provide some insight into how an individual that is planning to become a property investor or those who have already started with the journey of being property investors. It shall highlight the process for different strategies, the need to establish the company that would be used to buy, rent, or sell properties, provide advice on partnerships that can be established on the grounds of long term investment, look at the goal-setting (short, medium, and long-term goals) towards achieving financial freedom through property investment. Moreover, to describe what is meant by distressed properties and distressed property owners, the establishment of the property investment professional team, demonstrate how to source these distressed properties, unpack the risk of not having a mentor, and provide details of which investment structure (company, trust) one can use for the attainment of their properties.

All the information provided here by the author is based on the author's property investment experience, mentorship pieces of training that the author has conducted, books that the author has read, and interactions with the author's property investor mentees. However, it can't be emphasized enough that even if you have read this book, you still need to have a Mentor who will guide you accordingly, as it doesn't cover all the details that meet an individual's specific needs.

Chapter 1: Why You Should Invest in Property

There are many investment avenues that people can invest in, including but not limited to: stocks, bonds, shares, and other forms of investment. But there is something quite comforting about having an asset that you can touch and feel in comparison to something virtual. In fact, 90% of people become millionaires through investing in real estate. When you invest in real estate, you know where your property is situated and that it won't go anywhere unless it is an act of God or bombed. Property is a basic need for all humankind – therefore, no matter what's the economic situation is, there is always a need for shelter. You can buy and own it, or you can lease it depending on your situation.

Property is a tangible asset and is immovable. There are limited barriers to entry since anyone can own a property. Most importantly, property appreciates and generates equity, which can be used for re-investment. Therefore, if you invest creatively, you will have high returns on your investment (more than 15% profit in less than one year, particularly when you are using the house flipping strategy). The beauty of investing in property is that you have control over your investments; however, what should be noted is that you make money only when you buy the property, not when you sell. This statement means that when you buy below market value, you make a profit for both rentals, selling, or refinancing purposes.

Property investment provides you with financial freedom, free time to spend with your loved ones and do whatever you may desire. Leverage is one of the critical aspects when investing in the property business; you can leverage other people's money, time, and expertise. Lastly, if you have a property business, you can experience more tax benefits (e.g. depreciation, repairs, and maintenance, etc.) and pay yourself first.

It doesn't matter whether you are studying, working, or establishing your own company. The most important driving factor should be your big WHY. Ask yourself, why do you want to invest? Is it either for your time, financial freedom, or both (or anything else)? What is the problem that you are trying to solve? Lastly, ask yourself, what would happen if you won't achieve those goals that you have set for yourself?

When you are planning to invest in real estate, you need to treat it as a business so that you can be able to grow it and see results. This would assist you in the future to take advantage of using other people's time, money, and expertise, as Robert Kiyosaki mentioned it in his book *Rich Dad Poor Dad*. If you have a business, it is easy to transfer it to your kids, helps you to acquire big loans from the lending institutions, and reduce your government tax. You can pay yourself first and incorporate all the expenses related to the management of the property (i.e. maintenance, repairs, salaries, municipal rates and taxes, insurance, levies, etc.).

Chapter 2: Skills Development

Skills development is one of the most critical aspects of financial wealth, no matter what level of self-growth you are at. Most of the people want to venture into business space but fail to take the right first step, which is to educate themselves. Once you have decided on starting any business, it is important to research as well as identify training requirements for whatever you want to venture in.

In the property investment business, the most important skills you need to acquire are knowledge of how to use a computer, particularly the use of e-mails, Microsoft Excel, the internet, followed by reading and listening to property investment books. There are many books available online (i.e. Amazon); others are available at the libraries and local bookstore or other outlets located in South Africa. This book has a recommended list of some books that the reader can find to enhance their level of knowledge, which can be found towards the end of the book. As an entrepreneur, you need to read at least five pages from the book every day.

One of the challenges that most people face is the lack of knowledge as to where they may source suitable material that would help them to learn more about the business that they want to venture in. Some spend too much time on social media not to learn but to read people's gossip. Therefore, as you read this book, I recommend that you use social media as one of the sources where you can gather knowledge by joining groups that are related to your business and associate with friends that share the same vision as you.

Times have changed; most businesses use free physical seminars and live webinars as marketing tools. Attending seminars and webinars is important for learning purposes and networking. However, the knowledge that one can get from attending these seminars is not sufficient; hence the need to get a mentor that will assist you in bridging or closing the gap from no experience to almost knowledgeable. It is recommended that you attend one seminar or live webinar quarterly.

Chapter 3: The Power of Having a Mentor

I believe that all of us had mentors during our childhood years, which were our parents/guardians, or any elders in our communities. As we grew up, we went to school and teachers, together with our parents, were our mentors. After completion of tertiary education, we entered the working space, and once again, our line managers became our mentors.

However, most of the people venture into entrepreneurship simply decided to work on their own without anyone's guidance. Unfortunately, this attitude has resulted in the failure for most of the new businesses within the period of their first two years of establishment, globally. The question we should ask ourselves is, why do we think that being an entrepreneur is different from the above-mentioned phases that we went through to be successful and to be where we are now? I believe that if you learn from someone who has been there and done it before, you could accelerate your chances of success compared to someone who starts from level zero without the knowledge, experience, and mentor.

My advice is that once you have decided to pursue a property business or any business for that matter, the first step would be to have a mentor. Such a person would assist you in developing your short, medium, and long-term property investment goals (as discussed in the following chapter). Your mentor should be able to advise you on different property investment strategies that you should apply to achieve your goals based on your knowledge, experience, and financial capacity. Your mentor shall guide and motivates you and introduce you to his or her property investment networks. Consequently, it will assist you in reaching your goals quicker, depending on your willingness to be coached and your commitment to working hard.

Your mentor shall assist you in establishing your property investment professional team (see details of your team responsibilities in the following chapter). Also, help you in doing a proper property market analysis so that you can make informed decisions when you invest. Don't be afraid to leverage other people's money (OPM) and other people's time (OPT). Lastly, don't be afraid to use debt so that you can grow your portfolio quicker.

Chapter 4: Roles and Responsibilities of a Mentor and Mentee

Mentoring can be used in a wide range of settings as an effective intervention process to make the most of an individual's potential. It is often delivered in business, education, sport, or similar context where the focus is to support and help the mentee overcome specific difficulties or a range of difficulties. Mentoring can also be used to support and encourage people to manage their learning so that they may maximize their potential, develop their skills, improve their performance, and become the person they want to be.

A mentor should always strive to provide non-judgmental support, enables and empowers a mentee to identify and commit to a process of positive change. Equipped with relevant knowledge and expertise, the mentor assists the mentee on both a practical and personal level in achieving goals, which will eventually lead to long term success or greater happiness.

To achieve the desired goals and success, a mentor must set ground rules up front. These ground rules shall highlight the following:

- ⇒ Ensure there is a clear understanding of the purpose and parameters of the mentoring relationship.
- ⇒ Establish rules and boundaries.
- ⇒ Agree on aims/goals at the outset of the process.
- ⇒ Be consistent, reliable, and establish a good rapport.
- ⇒ Be prepared, open-minded, and open-hearted for your meetings.
- ⇒ Make each session positive and fun!
- ⇒ Prepare for a positive ending from the start.
- ⇒ Review and provide feedback progress at the end of each session.
- ⇒ Confidentiality. A part of mentoring is sharing the fears, sins, and scars of your soul. So, it's important that you establish a relationship of trust by committing to mutual confidentiality.
- ⇒ Have a clear time frame. Most of the time, when two people enter into a mentoring relationship, they neglect to discuss a time frame for

the relationship. So, from the very start, discuss not only the frequency of your meetings but agree to have a start date and an end date for the mentoring relationship.
⇒ Two-way learning conversations, as this is a mutual learning experience.
⇒ Agree upon a specific process or plan. Most mentoring fail because of lack of process or plan to follow. The first meeting or two go well as people get to know each other. But after that, neither of them knows where to go from there. So, from the beginning, discuss what the mentoring time will look like and what development needs you will focus on.
⇒ Periodic evaluation of the mentor relationship. Not all mentoring relationships work. And that is okay. That's why it's important to evaluate the relationship on occasion to make sure you're not wasting each other's time.
⇒ Establish a time frame. For a formal mentor program, time frames typically last for six months to a year. The goals that you establish need to be consistent with the timing.
⇒ Plan regular meetings. Have these scheduled with an established agenda provided ahead of time?
⇒ Constructive feedback. Both sides of the arrangement need to be able to give and receive constructive feedback. The goal of having a mentor is to grow. If you cannot take the advice you are given, you won't.
⇒ Confidentiality. In a formal relationship, your mentor typically is not someone you report to (i.e. your boss). Any information the mentee provides the mentor (assuming everything is copacetic) needs to be held in confidence due to the nature of what the two of you may be discussing.

Your mentor is responsible for providing you with a set of roles and responsibilities that include but not limited to the following: weekly, monthly, and yearly tasks that are aligned with your short, medium, and long-term plan and strategies. Use every communication avenue provided to you by your mentor, but don't expect immediate responses from your mentor as he or she will respond within the agreed time frames.

Chapter 5: Setting Out Goals

As a mentor, I have come across many students who didn't have clarity as to why they were working or embarking on investing in the property business. The challenge is that most of us were never taught at school as to why we were studying, except that we needed to get a good job, climb the corporate ladder, buy a house and get married, save for retirement. Most people have never been taught that they should study and work to empower themselves so that in the future, they can have their own businesses, create employment, leave a legacy for their generations to come, and be financially independent.

As a mentee, you need to ask yourself what is your purpose, what is it that you want to achieve, and what would happen if you don't achieve those goals that you have set for yourself? Most importantly, you need to be willing to unlearn what you have learned, develop a positive mental attitude, think big, work hard, be self-driven, network, develop new habits (read books that are aligned with your strategies), and surround yourself with like-minded people that will assist you to reach your goals.

Most of the people, when asked how much they would like to earn per month that would make them feel financially independent, wouldn't answer this. Instead, they would look at their current situation and simply say – whatever that would make me not to wake up in the morning and go to work. As you can see, there is a lack of clarity as to how much (the number) they want. In most cases, they don't even know when (time frame) they would achieve that goal, let alone the strategies to arrive there.

When you are setting goals, they must be SMART (specific, measurable, attainable, and time-based), and you must believe that you can achieve them before anyone else can believe you. Even if you have set them, you must also establish some strategies, tactics, and processes to attain those goals. Even if you have done everything above, but don't take action and be committed to attaining them, they would never materialize. Most importantly, there must be something huge that drives you to set these goals – your BIG

WHY. Why do you want to be successful, what makes you not to sleep at night?

Normally, when I advise my students, I ask them not to look at their background or current situation and determine their future. Instead, to look at themselves as that person or lifestyle they aspire to live, say in 10 years to come. However, as you know that you have to start somewhere, analyze your current financial situation and determine how you can optimize it to propel you to your desired goals.

Note that budgeting is critical in everyone's daily life; therefore, start by listing everything that you would like to have, e.g. house, car, education, vacations, fuel, gym, grocery, clothing, entertainment, etc. After you have listed these, put the price on them, e.g. house worth R5 000 000 and then reduce it to monthly expenses, say R50 000. Do this to all items you have listed and obtain the total. Let's say your total comes to R 300 000 per month. Therefore, this R300 000 means that you need properties that will generate this amount per month, which would be 10% of your total monthly revenue that equates to R3 000 000. Assume that a 2x bedroom house will cost you R450 000 to construct and then divide it by R6000 for a monthly rental, which will then give you some units that you need, and it is 500 units. Once you have determined the number of units, distribute that number within a certain period, i.e. 10 years (3-year intervals) that you have pre-set to meet your financial independence.

Once you have set all the number of properties that you require to achieve your financial independence, determine strategies (e.g. house flipping, buy-to-let, developments, and/or refinancing) that you are going to apply per three-year intervals to meet your desired goal. All of this depends on your financial capability, property investment knowledge and experience, commitment, and taking action once the opportunity presents itself. In the following chapter, we will dive deep into the abovementioned strategies. This book will cover the step-by-step guideline for the following strategies:
- ⇒ House flipping.
- ⇒ Buy-to-let.

- ⇒ Rent-to-own.
- ⇒ Rent-to-rent.
- ⇒ Multi-let.
- ⇒ Installment sale (owner financing strategy).
- ⇒ Refinancing strategy.
- ⇒ Buying from Sheriff's auction.
- ⇒ Buying from a private auction.
- ⇒ Foreclosure.
- ⇒ Land subdivision.
- ⇒ Consolidation.

Chapter 6: Exit Strategies

One thing that is fascinating about property business is that if you have made a good decision when you buy, it would not matter how the economy performs. What really matters is that people will always need a roof over their heads. However, as the property investor, you need to be able to monitor the performance of your investment because if you don't, you will end up losing everything. Most importantly, you need to establish your exit strategies before you even sign the offer to purchase and also make sure that you analyze them thoroughly.

It is, therefore, recommended that whenever you invest your money in any kind of business, you need to have an exit strategy. The exit strategy is any mechanism that you will use to minimize the loss of your investment, particularly if your preferred strategy is no longer financially viable. There are several exit strategies that one can use, depending on an individual's preference and circumstances; these strategies include but not limited to selling, renting, and leasing. We are now going to look at house flipping (buy-to-sell) strategy and apply the other exist strategies to provide some meaning to it.

Renting Strategy – Single let or Multi-lets or student lets

Here we go, let's say you bought a distressed freestanding house intending to refurbish and sell it. However, due to property market conditions, the property takes longer to be sold and is starting to be a liability to you. Your first exit-strategy could be to rent it out and get a monthly rental for a certain period until there are changes on the market. Nonetheless, you need to decide whether you will do a single rental (renting out the entire house to one family or person) or multi-lets (renting out per room and have multiple tenants in one house where they share the kitchen and bathroom). The last one would be to rent it out to students where you will be renting out per bed (depending on the size of the rooms, you may have two beds per room) to maximize your cash flow. Therefore, in conclusion, when you buy a property, you must have an end in mind (assess whether you will make a profit when you sell or rent it out), and you must have an exit strategy (Plan B) in place.

Leasing strategy – Control over the property

Using the same property above, we now look at the leasing option. In this option as the investor, you decide to lease out your property outright (the lessee has control over the property and is responsible for the payment of rates, water, electricity, maintenance, repairs, insurance, and any other costs associated with the property except the bond).

Leasing strategy – Airbnb

The second leasing strategy is the new one called Air Beds & Breakfast (Airbnb), which is a marketplace that connects travelers with local property owners online. This is for the travelers who visit the city and don't want to stay in a hotel or hostel. It gives you many choices from which you can easily book a room or an apartment. In this strategy, you as the owner are responsible for everything (payment of rates, maintenance, repairs, insurance, installation of the furniture, water, electricity, cleaning, bond repayment, and any other costs associated with the property) and you pay a certain percentage to the software company that facilitates the whole process.

Chapter 7: Comparative Market Analysis

It is critical that you conduct property economic analysis or risk assessment. In this analysis, you need to include the area where you will be investing, the market that you want to serve, types of properties you want to invest in, and, lastly, to decide on the price range of the properties that you want to buy and sell.

Area

As you might have heard, the location is very important when it comes to property investment. However, oftentimes we only focus on the location and forget to assess the area: whether it has a good annual gross yield (should not be less than at least 15%), vacancy rate (of not more than at least 7%) for rental purposes. Also, when you are flipping houses, check whether you will be able to sell fast (not more than 3 months on the market), or it stays in the market to the point where you will sell at a loss.

Targeted market

Decide on your target market, whether you want to invest in properties that will accommodate students (consider the proximity to the learning institutions, security, etc.), young single professionals, families, or old age home. Most importantly, as an investor, you should understand that the demand for a certain area is different from another; therefore, one-size-fits-all doesn't work in the property business.

Property types

Furthermore, you need to think about the type of properties that you want to invest in, for example: flats (bachelor flats, one bedroom, two bedrooms flat, or three bedrooms flat), complex (simplex, duplex or triplex) commercial properties, retail, multi-use (the combination of residential, offices and retail), freestanding houses, or the combination thereof.

Price range

Moreover, you need to decide on the price range of the properties that you want to invest in. Those that are in demand can be sold quicker if you are flipping. Also, decide on a rental price range if you are renting out your properties. My advice is that as a serious property investor, you should invest less on bachelor and one-bedroom flats because their exit strategies are not always favorable, i.e. you can't do the multi-let, and sometimes they take longer to appreciate for refinancing purposes and rental is restricted.

Chapter 8: Business Partnership

Depending on an individual's preferences, financial capacity, and complexity of certain projects, some investors would prefer to invest alone, whereas others prefer to work in partnerships (either family members, friends, and/or business partners). What is more important is that you need to decide as early as possible whether you are going to establish a company alone or you will have a partner or partners.

If you are planning to have partners, you must involve your partner in both training and strategic planning so that you can all be on the same level of understanding and also ensure that you draft legal agreements outlining each party's roles and responsibilities. More importantly, don't use your emotions when choosing your partner but conduct a risk assessment and understand how you both going to leverage on each other; it could be in terms of skills, capital, and time. Sometimes you may decide to do a once-off partnership for a certain project (joint venture). Despite everything, you MUST CHOOSE YOUR PARTNER CAREFULLY!!!

Chapter 9: Business Operating Structure

There are some structures that one can use to invest in real estate, which include but not limited to the following: individual capacity (buying properties under your name), LTD Company, and Trust. Let's look at an individual capacity structure; it is recommended as an initial structure that one can use.

The advantage of buying properties under your name is that it is easy to access funding from the traditional banks, provided that you have a job, you are earning a monthly salary, and you can afford according to the bank system. There are high possibilities of receiving a 100% bond from the bank, and you can receive a reasonable interest rate. If you are working for the government, you are entitled to further discount on your rate for your first house, provided that you are not buying it for rental but as your residential property.

The second one is the LTD Company. This one requires to be established as early as possible so that it could be used in the long term for purchasing and selling properties. The reason why it shall be established as early as possible is that the traditional banks normally require that you provide them with the three-year financial report so that they can assess the risk of funding it.

The advantages of buying properties using the company include but are not limited to tax benefits and all expenses (maintenance, repairs, rates, insurance, your salary, etc.) associated with the property would be taken into consideration during tax calculations. Whereas if you are buying under your name, any profit that you make will be taxed, and all items mentioned above would not be taken into consideration.

As for the Trust, it is recommended that you seek a legal trust expert to advise you with its requirements and maintenance thereof due to its complexity and cost associated with its maintenance. The beginners should start with the Ltd Company. Thereafter they can look at the Trust option. However, a Trust structure is highly recommended for long-term property investments (Buy-to-let strategy, development, and all paid up assets).

Chapter 10: Property Investment Professional Team

Your success depends on whom you associate with and surround you in terms of support. Therefore, to be successful as an entrepreneur or run any business successfully, one needs to have a team of people that can work with for the success of one's endeavors. Therefore, as a property investor, you don't have to do everything by yourself. As it was mentioned earlier in the book, you must use other people's time, expertise, and knowledge; hence you can focus on achieving your strategic plan. Below are some of the suggested team members you will need to succeed, as well as their brief responsibilities:

Team member	Role
Property Investment Mentor	Provides you with property investment knowledge, advice, guidance, support, motivation, and resources to meet your goals.
Bond Originator	Provides free bond application service with all major banks; hence you can get the best and cost-effective interest rates for your bond repayments.
Insurance broker	Deals with the sourcing of the best and cost-effective insurance from many insurers so that you can ensure that it will suit your need.
Contractor	Provides the services of constructing structures and maintenance of them as well as providing you with a cost estimate for construction and timeframes to complete it. They can also assist you when viewing properties.
Architect	Provides services of designs, the approval of designs, and management of the project.
Estate Agent	Provides you with services of rent, sell, or buy a property. They study property listings, interview prospective clients, and advice you accordingly for any selling, renting, and buying of properties in their respective area or town.
Sourcing Agent	Search for deals so that they can provide you with property deals that suit your requirements in exchange for a commission.

Financial Accountant	Provides you with services of developing financial models for business plan purposes and financial accounts (income statement, balance sheet, and cash flow statements).
Tax Accountant	Provides services related to tax and can assist you in tax compliance matters with SARS.
Transferring Attorney	Provides property transfer process, which includes registration of the bond and payments.
Lawyer specializing in evictions	Specialize in eviction matters.
Town Planner	Provides services for zoning application and advise you on municipal requirements regarding property matters and future developments.
Quantity Surveyor	Provides services of quantifying the cost estimate for the construction, which includes material, equipment, and human resources.
Land Surveyor	Provides services of a land survey, inserting boundaries of the site, and process the application of site subdivision.

Chapter 11: Property Buying Process Flow

You must only buy a property that has equity and buy from the distressed owners or buy a distressed property to make money because you make money when you buy! Don't use emotions when you buy a property but use numbers.

Buying a house is a long and tedious process for someone who is doing it for the first time. Nonetheless, this guide's objective is to provide guidance from the initial stage of buying a house, renting it out, and/or selling it. So, let us dive in… the first thing that one should think about is why you want to buy a property? Is it for a buy and hold strategy (to wait for it to appreciate then sell), or is it for the rental purpose (passive income) or flipping (active income)? Once you have decided on this, then you need to consider which structure you are going to use to buy. Is it under your personal name or the company or trust?

Funding strategy is critical: (although I recommend using other people's money, e.g. bank) are you going to buy using cash or the bond from the bank? If you are going to use a bank, it is advisable that you first visit a bond originator that would apply for the bond on your behalf to all the banks. As a result, you can save your time and get a bond pre-approval with a bank that provides you with better interest rates. A pre-approval certificate will provide you with important information, which includes the total amount you qualify for, the interest rates as well payback period. This information will assist you to know the maximum price of the property that you can buy.

You also need to consider the type of property that you want to buy based on your investment strategy (rental, flipping, or buy and hold). Is it going to be a flat, standalone (free standing), or a townhouse? Depending on your strategy and the target market, you need to consider space and number of rooms in the house to purchase. The area is one of the critical aspects when you buy a house; you need to do thorough research about the area where you want to invest. Make sure that the area has less crime, is close to either social and economic amenities, like schools, police stations, hospitals, public transport, and so on. Don't be afraid to ask the estate agent critical questions about the property and the area.

Once the abovementioned requirements have been met, start looking for your house to purchase either from listed properties, auctions, Gumtree, bank's repo websites (e.g. www.myroof.co.za), or any other avenue where properties are listed. If possible, advertise on Facebook for referrals. View as many properties as possible to find the best and during your viewing process, make sure that you collect as much information as possible that will assist you in making calculations and making an informed decision.

Once you have found a good deal (the property that will provide you with profit either for rental or resell), then sign an offer to purchase in which the estate agent will present it to the seller. Once the seller has accepted your offer, then you have purchased yourself a property, and then the transfer process will commence. Please note that the transfer process can take a minimum of 6 weeks, depending on the complexity of the deal and whether you are buying for cash (the process is much quicker and short) or using a bank bond. After the transfer process is completed, you will receive your title deed if paid cash. And if you used a bond, you will only receive your title deed once you have paid up your bond.

Chapter 12: Property Selling Process Flow

As mentioned in the previous chapter, you only make money when you buy, not when you sell. Based on your initial applied investment strategy, you are now executing an exit strategy, which is to sell your property. The aim is to make sure that you receive a profit out of all properties that you are selling or that you will be selling going forward.

Let's assume that you bought your property below market value and you have increased its value by doing the refurbishments and some necessary expansions. The first step to take would be to evaluate your property to determine its current market value (selling price). This can be done by comparing similar properties that are listed on your national property listing platform as well as on the national platform for previously sold properties to get an average price (this would have been done when you purchase the property as well, on your calculations).

Importantly, you need to have a price range (minimum and maximum offers that you can accept, e.g. R900 000 minimum to R1 100 000 maximum). Your minimum price must give you a profit of at least 10%, and the maximum price can be anything above 20% of profit (to be used as your initial listing price). This price range will assist you when it comes to negotiations, particularly when a potential buyer is willing to buy a property but can't afford a maximum price.

Once you have determined a selling price, you need to decide on your selling strategy. There are three types of selling strategies that you may use, which include but not limited to Sole Mandate, Executive Mandate, Open Mandate as well as listing and selling it yourself (not recommended).

Sole Mandate is whereby you, as a seller, appoint one and only one Estate Agent to list and sell your property. The disadvantage of this strategy is that if anyone, including yourself, can find a buyer, the appointed Estate Agent would still be eligible for the commission. Another disadvantage is that your property would be listed in some of the platforms, which the Estate Agent is not subscribed to, which would reduce the reach to a bigger market. However, you may use this strategy at your advantage by negotiating small commission fees, which you will have to pay an Estate Agent once the property is sold.

Let's look at the **Executive Mandate**. In this strategy, you select at least more than two Estate Agents that can sell your property. The commission would only be received by the Estate Agent who has managed to find a buyer first and would take all the commission. The advantage of using this strategy is that your property would be listed in more platforms, and the reach to the market is better than the Sole Mandate.

Open Mandate is whereby you as a seller have selected an unlimited number of Estate Agents that can list and sell your property, including yourself (if you find a buyer you would have saved the commission fee that you would have paid to an Estate Agent). The advantage of using this strategy is that you can negotiate for a lesser commission fee, and your property would be advertised on many platforms where many people would see it. The disadvantage would be access to the property as all these estate agents would call you now and then to access the property, for viewing purposes.

In addition to the selection of the selling strategy, you should decide on who would be your transferring attorney since it's your responsibility to do so, not the buyers. Therefore, it's better to have a transferring attorney among your mastermind team that would often advise you accordingly, in property legal matters, and for free since you would bring deals to him or her.

Once all the above-mentioned processes have been completed, you will then have to wait for the offers. As you have your price range, you will only consider offers that are within it, and when you find a good deal, you will sign the offer to purchase. Once the offer to purchase has been signed by both parties (seller and the buyer), then your estate agent shall contact your transferring attorney and start with the transferring process up until it is concluded. Afterwards, the property is no longer under your name and, thereafter, receive all your monies.

Chapter 13: Property Viewing

Viewing and inspection of the property are one of the most critical aspects of investing in real estate because one mistake can cost you tens of thousands of rands. Therefore, before you commit yourself to any deal, you must view the property personally and do a thorough inspection so that you can be able to determine possible refurbishment cost, which will assist you in calculating the minimum price at which you can purchase it and make a profit at the end of the deal.

When you inspect the property, it is recommended to bring along an experienced contractor to help you, if you don't have experience and expertise. Note that you can request an estate agent to view the property. Then follow by the inspection (firstly, go alone to view the property, and if you see that there are too many things that need to be fixed, then during the second visit, you should bring along your contractor to do the inspection).

The most important thing when you go to view the property is to prepare a list of questions that you will have to ask the estate agent. Below is a typical list of questions that you should ask, which include but not limited to the following:

⇒ Why is the owner selling? This question will assist you in getting an understanding of whether the seller is motivated to negotiate the selling price or not.
⇒ What exactly is included in the sale? Don't assume that the exquisite chandelier will be staying - insist that everything being removed is documented in the sales agreement.
⇒ How long has the property been on the market? Overpriced homes tend to stay on the market for longer than realistically priced homes do.
⇒ How long have the present owners lived there? This question will assist you in understanding if the property has some challenges in case the owners haven't stayed for more than one year. A follow-up question should be why they stayed for a short period, which then

leads you to understand if the property in question has some problems (structurally, neighborhood, crime, and so forth).
⇒ What is the minimum price the seller will accept? Buyers should never assume that every seller is open to offers. Finding out how much the seller will be willing to accept to part with his property will save both the buyer and seller a great deal of time and could obviate third parties intervening with their offers while your negotiations are underway.
⇒ What offers have there been so far? Based on this question and the one that asks how long has the property been on the market, you would understand how motivated and frustrated the owner is.
⇒ When do the sellers have to move out? Again, this is tremendously important and should be documented along with a stipulated sum of occupational rent if the buyer is planning to move in before transfer takes place.
⇒ Has any major work been done to the property, or have any of the rooms been refurbished recently? And if so, why? If the answer is yes and the work has been completed, have the plans been updated and approved by the local municipality/ authority?
⇒ Are plans available for the property? It is highly recommended that buyers insist on a clause in the sales agreement in which the seller warrants that municipal plans are in order.
⇒ Ask if you can take a picture of the house and if you can, move the furniture to look underneath.
⇒ Ask about the neighbors: if they are noisy or not, public transport, police station, and other amenities in close proximity to the property.
⇒ Will the sellers agree to a home inspection? If not, why? A home inspection is not mandatory at this stage, but it is always wise to hire a home inspector before signing a sales agreement. Sellers who object could be doing so because they are aware of major flaws in the home. They will also be aware that if the flaw is serious, it could affect the asking price.
⇒ It is also important to ask about the monthly municipal rates and taxes, average electricity consumption, and levies if it's a sectional

title. Also, if it's a sectional title, ask about the financials of the complex, whether they are still up to date.

When viewing the property, make sure that you bring along an inspection checklist so that you can be able to note all the defects (rate them as follows: poor, average, and excellent). Make sure that you focus on the defects and ask more about them so that you can create an impression to the estate agent that the asking price might not be met when you submit your offer to purchase. Your inspection checklist must cover the outside of the house (fence, landscape, lawn, driveway, painting, roof, walls, foundation, drainage, storm water, plumbing, and neighborhood) and end with the inside of all the rooms (painting, ceiling, walls, lights, light switches, plugs, taps, doors, cardboards, floor, geyser, stove). Below is an example of a checklist inspection form to use when viewing the property, and it will assist you to estimate the costs of refurbishment and build your case for negotiation phase:

Item No.	Item Description	Excellent	Good	Poor	Remarks
1	Driveway				
2	Fence				
3	Drainage				
4	Roof				
5	Swimming pool				
6	Garden				
7	Exterior wall painting				
8	Terrain				
9	Garage door(s)				
10	Doors and Windows				

Chapter 14: Property Financing

Finance is one of the critical aspects when it comes to the property business. Nevertheless, there are now numerous ways in which one can be able to own or buy a property, which include but are not limited to the following:

- ⇒ The first one is to apply for the bond from the traditional banks and other government lending institutions.
- ⇒ The second one is the use of your own savings.
- ⇒ Joint venture - where you partner with someone on a specific project with the purpose of sharing the responsibilities, resources, skills, and profit.
- ⇒ Stokvel - where like-minded people meet and contribute money (once-off or monthly or annually) with the main purpose of investing in real estate.
- ⇒ Find an angel investor - when you find an investor to invest capital in your project, usually for the purpose of exchanging for debt or ownership equity.
- ⇒ Property refinancing – this is when you have an existing property that is paid up or has generated equity, or you have built it from scratch; thus it has increased in terms of the market value, then you apply for the access equity and reinvest it to buy other properties.
- ⇒ Bridging finance – this is a fund that you can borrow from other landing institutions to close the gap between the total bond (90% bond) from the bank the 10% deposit.

It is highly recommended that you don't use your own money when investing in property but use other people's money. Keep your money so that you can use it to pay for the transfer and bond registration costs that will be required to complete the process of buying a property.

As an individual or partner, you will need to decide on how you will raise capital, whether it can be cash from your own savings or the bond from the bank, joint venture, or private funders. If you are buying a property for the first time and it's less than R900 000, it is advisable to buy it under an individual's personal name, but it must be registered as your residence, not for rentals. Moreover, when you approach the banks for the bond, they will only request for your three-months bank statement and your payslip. Whereas, if you buy under company name, you will need both your personal information and the company's financial standing. However, you can buy under the company name if you will be paying cash.

The best way to obtain the bond from the banks will be to approach the bond originator (this service is for free) who will, on your behalf, apply for the funding to all the banks in your country. Once the application results are back from the banks, you shall choose one bank with the best offer. Thereafter you will be provided with a bond pre-approval certificate. This certificate will entail the amount in which you are qualified to purchase for, the interest rate that you will pay, and whether you will be required to pay a deposit or not.

When you apply for the bond from the bank using your company, please note that the banks are not risk-takers; therefore, they only consider bond applications from a company that has been trading for more than two years and has healthy financials. You would also have to budget for a minimum of 10% as a deposit, together with bond registration and transfer costs.

Chapter 15: Sourcing of Distressed Properties

Sourcing of distressed properties depends on an individual's choice of either being a one-person operation (OMO) or using other people's time (OPT). Nonetheless, it is recommended that the OPT method is applied so that you can focus on the management of the company and on analyzing deals because time is money! There are several ways in which deals can be sourced by using methods that include but not limited to the following:

⇒ An internet search for listed properties and advertisements on social media.
⇒ Referrals by people that know you personally or know what you do.
⇒ Driving around the neighborhood to identify de-stressed properties.
⇒ Other People's Time (OPT) method, which includes but not limited to the following:
⇒ Sourcing agents – they drive around to look for good deals and negotiate on your behalf in exchange for a commission.
⇒ Wholesalers – they buy from the auction and sell to you or on your behalf (provide them with the power of attorney letter) for commission purpose.
⇒ When you attend property network sessions.
⇒ Sheriff Auctions.
⇒ Private Auctions.
⇒ My Roof website.
⇒ Divorce Attorneys.
⇒ Deceased Estates Attorneys.
⇒ Letting Agents.
⇒ Estate Agents.
⇒ Look out for signs where the owners sell the houses by themselves.
⇒ Bank repossession websites.

Chapter 16: Buying from Private Auction

Here, the property investor attends and participates in an auction with an intension to buy the property below the market value. The seller advertises to sell his or her property on auction with the intention to attract more buyers and increase the chances of selling it higher than the market value. Normally, the seller sets a minimum-selling price for the property for which the bidders must bid against. Once the winning bid has been achieved, the seller has the right to accept or reject it.

Step 1: *Collection of information:* Make sure that you have all details about the property that would be auctioned, these include:
- ⇒ Auction date.
- ⇒ Auction venue.
- ⇒ Location of the property.
- ⇒ Time.
- ⇒ Name of the auctioneer.
- ⇒ Required registration fee and read all the requirements so that you are ready.

Step 2: *Property Viewing*: The most important and critical step is to arrange with the auctioneer's estate agent to view the property. During the viewing proceedings, make sure that you have your inspection list, camera to take pictures, and ask questions (see a list of questions from the previous chapter) that will assist you in preparing your calculations. Make sure that on your inspection checklist you score each item according to the condition it is in, i.e. poor, good, or excellent. You may use numbers: 1 = poor; 2 = good; 3 = excellent.

During this process, make sure that you make the estate agent aware of the defects that you have observed and do not allow an estate agent to lead you because, in most cases, he or she will only show the items that are in good or excellent condition. By doing so, you are already planting in his or her mind that your offer will not be what might be expected based on their reserve price (minimum price in which the seller is willing to sell the property). This process will also assist you to be able to establish the refurbishment costs if applicable. If you realize that there are too many defects, ask the agent if you could come for the second viewing so that you can bring along your experienced contractor to do the inspection and provide you with accurate refurbishment cost estimates.

Step 3: *Running numbers:* Once you have viewed the property and gathered all the information that you need, you may start doing calculations (as mentioned earlier that we don't use emotions but numbers when buying property) so that you can determine the minimum and maximum price that you can purchase the property for. Remember, when you invest in property, the aim is to make a profit (minimum of 15%). When you resell it, or if you will be renting it out, it must make a profit from the first month as opposed to when the property appreciates in value.

In your calculations, you must make sure that you incorporate all the costs that you will incur during the purchase phase, refurbishment or rehabilitation phase, and reselling phase.

- ⇒ The purchase phase includes the following costs: transfer costs, auctioneer's commission fee, and bond registration fee if applicable. To calculate the transfer and bond costs, you can use the Ooba App.
- ⇒ Refurbishment phase includes the following costs: municipality rates and taxes, water, electricity, insurance, bond repayment if applicable, refurbishment costs, garden services, and levies if applicable.
- ⇒ The reselling phase includes the following costs: Estate agent commission and compliance certificates if applicable.

Your final offer to purchase should be calculated as follows: done up value (DUV) price, less purchase phase costs (PPC) + refurbishment phase costs (FPC) + profit (P) + reselling phase costs (RPC).

Formula: OTP = DUV -(PPC+FPC+P+RPC)

Step 4: *Attend auction*: Attend the auction on the set date and arrive 30 minutes before time. Bring along FICA documents (certified ID copy, proof of address not older than 3 months, and company documents if you will be purchasing using the company). If your funds would be obtained from the bank, bring along your bond pre-approval certificate as well as a bidding registration fee (refundable if you didn't win the bid). Check whether it will be cash or cheque and arrange accordingly. Once you have finished with the registration, you will receive the bidding board that you will use to indicate that you are interested in buying at the said bidding price.

Step 5: *Bid proceeding*: During the bidding proceeding, the auctioneer shall read out the rules and confirm all the details about the property, and thereafter the bidding commences. Based on your calculations, you would have prepared the minimum and maximum prices (price range) that you would use as your guide. Make sure that you don't exceed your maximum price because if you do, you will run a risk of purchasing a non-profitable property.

Step 6: *Winning a bid*: If you become lucky and win the bid, you will then engage with the auctioneer and sign the documents. However, this doesn't mean that your bid has been approved yet as it will be taken to the seller for approval, which takes a few days before you receive the outcome. If it is not approved, you will receive back your registration fee, and it might be open for negotiation. However, if your bid is approved by the seller, you will not receive back your registration fee, but it shall form part of the deal. The auctioneer will contact you and send you the offer to purchase (OTP) agreement, which you will need to sign and pay all the required monies as per the OTP. Then you shall make payments according to the stipulated time frames.

Step 7: *Signing the Offer to Purchase(OTP)*: Property transfer and registration process. Once the OTP has been signed by both the seller and yourself, you will be required to pay a deposit as well as to make payment for the appointment of the conveyancer. He will be responsible for the transfer of the property from the seller's name to your name or your company's name, whichever is applicable, as well as the bond registration attorney if you have received the bond from the bank.

Step 8: *Transfer of the property*: Depending on the appointed conveyancer as well the bond registration attorney (appointed by the bank) and lodgment at the deeds office, the entire registration process can take a minimum of 6 weeks or more. Once the registration process has been concluded, you will receive the agreement if you have used the bond to acquire the property or receive a title deed if you've paid for it in cash.

Step 9: *Post-registration*: Once the property has been registered under your name or company's name, you will now be responsible for everything regarding that property. This means that you will have to get property insurance, pay for municipality rates and taxes, levies (if it's a sectional title property), electricity, and the maintenance thereof.

Step 10: *Strategy implementation:* Now that you have the property, what is your next step? This depends entirely on the strategy that you initially set: whether you are going to flip it or rent it out as a single let or multi-lets, turn it into student accommodation, or extend it, it's up to you.

Chapter 17: Buying from the Sheriff's Auction

Here the property investor attends and participates in an auction with an intension to buy the property less than the market value. Properties are listed and published on Green Gazette to be sold on Sheriff in order to recover monies owed by the owner of the property. Normally, the Sheriff will give some information about the property, then ask the bidders to bid, and the highest bidder wins. Once the bidder has successfully won the bid, a deposit of 10% of the bidding price must be paid immediately, as well as the Sheriff's commission. Also, the balance of the money must be paid within the prescribed period set by the Sheriff.

Step 1: *Collection of information*: This step is similar to the one described on private auction, except that you only get the information when you have subscribed to the ShiriffHQ website (www.sheriffHQ.co.za). You can subscribe either for residential properties only or for commercial properties only or for both. There are two ways to receive the information, which are as follows: one is free and the other one is payable; for the free one, you subscribe to receive information for only two suburbs, and if you subscribed for the payable one, you can receive information for more than two suburbs, which also contain more information on the property.

Note that all information is not available here compared to the private auction, i.e. you will have to do your own research in terms of finding out the outstanding rates and taxes, outstanding bond payments, and levies if it's a sectional title property.

Step 2: *Property viewing:* It is not guaranteed that you will have access to view the property compared to the private auction because some owners or occupants will not provide you with access. Just imagine someone coming to your house saying that he is coming to view your property since it will be auctioned. Therefore, you must make means to view it from outside and do your observations and calculate estimates to determine if it requires some refurbishments.

Step 3: *Running numbers:* The way to calculate an offer to purchase the property for sheriff auction properties is similar to the one mentioned in the private auction strategy. However, the only difference between private auction and sheriff auction is that the following costs are not given, and you have to do your homework to get them. This includes municipal rates and taxes, levies if it's a sectional title property, water, and electricity. If you don't take these costs into account during your calculation, you will find yourself in trouble having to pay more than what the property will worth.

Step 4: *Bid proceeding*: Sheriff auction bidding procedure is similar to private auction one. The only difference between the sheriff and private auction is that once you have won the bid, the property becomes yours immediately, including all the costs associated with it as long as you will be able to pay for all the costs. Once you have signed the paperwork with the sheriff, you will have to contact the transferring attorney that has been assigned to that property so that you may start with the transfer process.

Chapter 18: Foreclosure

Foreclosure (buying a property before it goes on auction) is a strategy whereby a property investor negotiates with the distressed property owner. In this situation, the property is already listed for public auction, and the date for the auction is already set. As a creative investor, you intend to buy it before it can be auctioned to avoid competition and to assist the owner to mitigate the risk of being blacklisted and lose the property altogether. The property must possess high equity as a deciding factor to purchase it. For this strategy to be a success, you must only pay with cash and work with your mentor.

Step 1: *Subscription:* Subscribe to your national sheriff website if it's available (i.e. www.sheriffHQ.co.za); this website provides all listed properties for auction per area or suburb in South Africa.

Step 2: *Investment areas*: Choose at least three areas in which you would like to invest in so that you will receive listed properties in those areas.

Step 3: *Type of investment properties*: Once you have received this information, decide on which properties you would like to purchase based on the type of properties that you want (these can include the number of bedrooms, standalone house, or an apartment or a townhouse).

Step 4: *Desktop research:* Before you go and view each property, do your desktop research and the calculations to determine the current market value of the property, how much equity is available, outstanding bond fees, outstanding rates, and taxes as well as levies if applicable.

Step 5: *Contact the owner:* Now that you have some information about the property, contact the owner either by SMS, email, phone call. You can also place a postcard with all your contact details in the post box or doorstep and just knock at the door, introduce yourself, and explain why you are there. Contact details of the owner can be found by subscribing to your national platform that captures information for all properties that have been registered with your local deeds office.

Step 6: *Meeting and collection of information:* If the owner is available for a meeting, start by telling the owner about your business and what you do before you talk about his or her challenges with regards to the property so that he or she can trust you and open up to you. Talk more about how you can assist the owner to avoid being blacklisted and the house being repossessed and sold on auction for less than what he or she is owing to the bank. Then he will end up having to pay a shortfall if the house is sold for less than the current loan balance. Ask if you can view the property so that you can see the amount of work that needs to be done in order to determine how much you can buy it for. Meanwhile, also make sure that you provide them with something to start their lives afresh.

Step 7: *Sign-off the offer to purchase:* You must make sure that you discuss the offer immediately after you have viewed the property and present your offer. You must have at least three offers (low, medium, and high) that you must present on site. Once you have agreed on the offer, you must sign the offer to purchase (you must prepare an offer to purchase document in advance and bring it with you). Please make sure that you state the date on which the owner must vacate the property, and that the payment will only be made once the owner has vacated the property within a specified date.

Step 8: *Contact the assigned transferring attorney* once you have signed the offer to purchase, which must include everything that you have agreed upon. Contact the transferring attorney (contact details would be available on listed property details) that has been assigned to sell the property and ask him or her to stop the property from going on auction on the set date. Then present the offer to purchase that has been signed by you and the owner. The attorney will then provide you with the bank details so that you can deposit the money under the stipulated period and sign all required documents.

Chapter 19: Refinancing

Property Refinancing Strategy is applicable only to properties that are registered under the municipality register, have approved drawings or plans, and enrolled under the National Housing Building Regulation Council (NHBRC) (if available in your country). There are four property categories in which this strategy can be applied. These include but not limited to a newly constructed property, upgraded or extended property, paid-up house, and a house that has appreciated in value over time and has an equity (the difference between the loan amount and current value of the property). In short, this strategy means that you re-bond your property or you request a second bond on the same property from the bank. If you qualify to apply for it, then the bank will approve 80% of your equity; e.g., let's say your equity is R500 000, then the bank will give you R400 000 as a second bond.

Let's assume that your property meets one of the above-mentioned categories, you have tenants in your property, and or your affordability is good. Then you should go to the bond originator who will assist you in preparing an application for a bond. The bond originator will then send the application to all the local banks. The response will come with different offers from these banks, and then you will have to choose the one with the best interest rate. In addition, if you find better rates from a different bank than yours, you should approach your bank and negotiate with them to provide similar rates.

Please use this strategy only if you are going to reinvest the money to buy more properties and grow your portfolio.

Chapter 20: House Flipping (Capital Flip)

House flipping refers to the purchase of the property (residential house) below the market value (at least less than 30% or higher) to sell it below market (at least less than 5% or below) to generate revenue. These properties can be purchased from the distressed sellers (relocating sellers, divorcees, listed for auction, retrenched, indebted, accidental landlord, on auction, etc.) or build and sell.

Step 1: *Partnership:* Decide whether you will work alone or as a partnership (to have a silent partner or make a joint venture).

Step 2: *Operating Structure:* You need to decide on the operating Structure that you will use to buy properties, would it be a Close Corporation(CC), Limited Company (PTY Ltd), or you will be buying under your name. If you are going to use either the CC or (Pty Ltd), you will need to register this structure with your national company registration entity and open a bank account for your structure. If you are starting and still working, it is recommended to use your name to buy properties since bank requirements are minimal (three-month bank statement, payslip, and proof of address) compared (three-year financials and personal financials) to that of the company. You may also use the combination of both personal name and the entity, especially when you are starting so that you can keep your entity active until you can be able to buy using it.

Step 3: *Establishment of a professional team:* To be successful, you need to establish a team that you will use to execute your projects. As mentioned earlier, you need to use other people's time and expertise. Your team should consist of the following members: mentor, contractor, estate agent, accountant, transferring attorney, architect, and town planner. As you are starting this journey, you will only utilize these members on an as and when required basis. The roles and responsibilities of these members are stated in the previous chapter.

Step 4: *Funding model:* Decide on a funding model that you will use to purchase the properties. Are you going to use cash or loan, which may come from the bank (bond, credit card, overdraft, and revolving loan), or private funders and loans from friends and family members? You can also use a combination.

Step 5: *Area analysis:* You must choose at least three areas or suburbs in which you will be investing in or flipping properties. These areas must have a potential for economic growth, which consists of new developments as well as sustainable economic activities. It must be near amenities, which include but not limited to public transport, schools, hospitals, police station, universities, and shopping centres. It is critical that you conduct thorough desktop research about the area and establish a good relationship with the estate agents around the area so that you may obtain more information from them with regards to the property market trend on these areas.

Step 6: *Type of deals:* As an investor, you must know your target market as to what type of properties you will deal with, which they would be able to sell fast. It's either you will focus on flats or apartments, stand-alone houses, or townhouses. Also, you need to decide as to how many bedroom houses you will buy: is it one bedroom, two, or more.

Step 7: *Sourcing of deals:* Decide on how you will source deals or look for properties. Are you going to utilize sourcing Agents (referrals) or Estate Agents, attend sheriff's auctions, private auctions, or buy foreclosures? Also, you can use a combination.

Step 8: *Viewing of properties:* Once the above planning is completed and all resources are in place, you can now start to identify and view properties that are aligned with your strategy. Make sure that you have an inspection checklist that you will be using during the viewing. It is important that during the viewing you are in control (ask as many relevant questions as possible), which will assist you in gathering necessary information that will help to make calculations and make an informed decision. You must ask the estate agent if it is allowed to come back again and do the inspection with your contractor to determine the refurbishment cost.

After you have done your calculations, put an offer. Remember that we don't use emotions but numbers when we buy and that we make money when we buy, not when we sell. Once your offer is accepted, the transfer process will commence. Bravo, you have yourself a property!

Chapter 21: Buy-to-let

The Buy-to-let strategy is whereby a property investor buys a property intending to rent it out to a single tenant to generate income (positive cash flow) for a long-term period. This strategy applies to student accommodation, families, professionals, and offices (depending on your target market, type of property, and the location).

Step 1: *Partnership:* Decide whether you will work alone or as a partnership (to have a silent partner or make a joint venture).

Step 2: *Operating Structure:* You need to decide on the operating Structure that you will use to buy properties: will it be a Close Corporation(CC), Limited Company (PTY Ltd), or your capacity. If you are going to use either the CC or (Pty Ltd), you will need to register this structure with your national company registration entity and open a bank account for your structure. If you are starting and still working, it is recommended to use your name to buy properties since bank requirements are minimal (three-month bank statement, payslip, and proof of address) compared to that of a company (three-year financials and personal financials). You may also use the combination of both personal name and the entity, especially when you are starting so that you can keep your entity active until you can be able to buy using it.

Step 3: *Establishment of a professional team:* To be successful, you need to establish a team that you will use to execute your projects. As mentioned previously, you need to use other people's time and expertise. Your team should consist of the following members: mentor, contractor, estate agent, accountant, transferring attorney, architect, and town planner. As you would be starting this journey, you will only utilize the team members on an as and when required basis. The roles and responsibilities of these members are stated in the previous chapter.

Step 4: *Funding model:* Decide on a funding model that you will use to purchase the properties. Are you going to use cash or loan, which may come from the bank (bond, credit card, overdraft, and revolving loan), private funders, or loans from friends and family members? You can also use a combination.

Step 5: *Area analysis:* You must choose at least three areas or suburbs in which you will be investing in or flipping properties. These areas must have a potential for economic growth, which consists of new developments, well established and sustainable economic activities. Also, it must be close to amenities, which include but not limited to public transport, schools, hospitals, police station, universities, and shopping centres. It is critical that you conduct thorough desktop research about the area and establish a good relationship with the estate agents in those areas so that you may obtain more information from them with regards to the property market trend on these areas.

Step 6: *Type of deals:* As an investor, you must know your target market as to what type of properties you will deal with, which they would be able to sell fast. It's either you will focus on flats or apartments, stand-alone houses, or townhouses. Also, you need to decide as to how many bedroom houses you will buy: is it one bedroom, two, or more.

Step 7: *Sourcing of deals:* Decide on how you will source deals or look for the properties. Are you going to use sourcing agents (referrals) or Estate Agents, attend sheriff's auctions, private auctions, buy foreclosures, or a combination?

Step 8: *Calculations:* When you are dealing with letting properties, you must make sure that you do proper calculations that will indicate whether you will make a profit or loss before you buy it. A financial model spreadsheet becomes critical in this regard because it allows you to populate in your investment capital, loan amount, together with the repayment period, as well as interest rate, expected monthly rental income, all the expenses (rates and taxes, insurance, maintenance costs, levies, property management cost by the letting agent, bank charges, etc.). After you have done these calculations, go and view properties. Remember that we don't use emotions when we buy a property, but we use numbers and that we make money when we buy, not when we sell or rent it out.

Step 9: *Viewing of properties:* Once the above planning is completed and all resources are in place, you may now start to look for and view properties that are aligned with your strategy. Make sure that you have an inspection checklist that you will be using during the viewing. It is important that during the viewing you are in control (you ask as many relevant questions as possible), which will assist you in gathering necessary information and will help you to do calculations and make an informed decision. You must ask the estate agent if it is allowed to come back again and do the inspection with your contractor to determine the refurbishment cost.

Step 10: *Appointment of a Letting Agent*: Once the registration and transfer process is concluded and the property is now under your name, assume that the refurb work is also completed and ready to be operational. Depending on an individual's plan, some people would prefer to manage and find the tenants by themselves; others would appoint a letting agent.

I recommend that you should appoint a letting agent to manage your property since they have experience and resources to deal with the management of property as well as tenants. As an investor, you must use other people's time and expertise so that you can find more deals and strategies to grow your portfolio.

I don't think you would appreciate to chase after tenants when they don't pay on time, let alone to be wakened up early in the morning for a blocked sewer; I don't want to even mention the eviction and screening of tenants. All you want is to receive your money at the end of the month from the letting agent. The cost for the management of the property is normally around 10% of your monthly total rent, which would have been considered before you buy a property.

Step 11: *Leasing of a property:* Once you have appointed your letting agent and you have signed the agreement, it is now the time for the agent to do their work. A letting agent's responsibility is to inform you how much you will be able to rent out your property for, in comparison with similar properties in the area. Advertise or list your property for rental. Once they find a potential tenant, they will do a background check (screening) to make sure that they lease a property to a good tenant who will be able to take care of your property and pay the rent according to the lease agreement.

It is the letting agent's responsibility to collect rent on your behalf, to fix any problems that might arise with regards to maintenance, and repair of the property. Your responsibility would be to pay for the repairs if they were not the tenant's cause. It is the responsibility of a letting agent to draft a lease agreement and make sure that it is signed by you and the tenant. Also, make sure that during the renewal of the lease agreement they take care of that.

Chapter 22: Multi-let Strategy

A multi-let strategy is when more than one tenant is renting or sharing one property (with two bedrooms and more) whereby they are renting one bedroom each and share the communal lounge, kitchen, and bathrooms. This strategy is good for high returns, positive cash flow, and high occupancy rate; it's ideal for students and the new working class.

The process of acquiring these properties is similar to the one illustrated in the previous chapter (buy-to-let strategy). Still, the only difference is that in buy-to-let you have a single-let (one person or one family is a tenant) whereas in multi-lets you have more than one tenants renting per room. The other difference between single and multi-lets is that in a single-let the tenant provides all the furniture whereas in a multi-let you as the landlord provide partial furniture in the living room.

The alternative for multi-let could be a student accommodation whereby you no longer rent out your property per room but per bed. In the student accommodation, you as the landlord provide furniture (beds, TV, fridge, microwave, couches, etc.), and students provide their bedding and other stuff they prefer to have compared to the ones provided. Depending on the size of the room and furniture set up, you may put two beds per room, and each student pay per bed. If someone wants to rent out the entire room, he or she will be liable to pay for both beds. With student accommodation, the landlord needs to make sure that there are strict rules governing how each student should behave and look after your property to avoid high maintenance costs for your property. Therefore, it is critical to request a deposit from each student so that if anything is damaged when they leave your property, you can retain that deposit and use it for repairs.

Chapter 23: Seller Financing Strategy (Installment Sale)

There are many creative property investment strategies that one can apply when wanting to invest in property – be it that you can qualify for the bond or not. Many of them have been explained in this book, and now we are going to look at a Seller Financing Strategy, better known as an Installment Strategy. However, it must be mentioned that it is not always easy to find properties that fall within this category. The reason is that most houses are usually being bonded, or the owner is not motivated enough to apply the strategy. Therefore, it is imperative that the house must be paid-up, and the owner must be highly motivated before this strategy can be applied.

In essence, Owner Financed Home Strategy is whereby a property investor buys a property (normally a paid-up house) from the owner with the intension to sell or lease it out. The strategy doesn't involve the use of the bank; sometimes if you negotiated well, there will be no deposit required, or you can pay a high deposit to better your chances during negotiations, there will be no credit check, etc. These properties can be identified by the signs installed outside the house that reads "FOR SALE BY THE OWNER or through word of mouth.

Once you see this sign, you must be excited because it means that you will be able to negotiate directly with the owner. This gives you a lavage to negotiate the interest rates to pay and the duration period in which you will pay off the property. So, once you have identified this property, do your desktop research and the calculations to determine how much you will buy this property for. Decide what you will use it for; is it going to be for rental or are going to flip it? It is recommended that even if your plan is to flip it, hold it for at least five years and rent it out so that the owner can be happy with you because he or she might have strong emotional attachments to it.

Most of the time, properties like these are found from owners that want to downsize from big houses and move to the old-age homes. Or maybe they are relocating or no longer have family members to stay with. Also, sometimes such properties can be found from accidental landlords (a person that has inherited a property but doesn't want it).

Chapter 24: Land Subdivision

There are many strategies available to make money in the property business as long as you have the know-how. Other strategies require less capital if you already have a site or you want to buy a new one. One of them is a land subdivision that can be applied to a new vacant site or an existing large site. Depending on the local municipality bylaws, a site can be site subdivided into several sites that meet the particular suburb zoning requirements (i.e. minimum site surface area to be not less than 1000m2).

Land Subdivision is a strategy that involves the purchase of land, land survey, and installation of services (water, sewer, roads, electricity, and stormwater) for sale purposes or you may exclude these services (less profit to make). The process includes the appointment of a development team, development of concepts studies, feasibility studies, business plan, financing, construction, and the sale of plots thereafter.

Step 1:   *Zoning requirements:* When you plan to apply this strategy, the first step is to appoint a Town Planner who will analyze the zoning for the site and determine whether the process of subdivision will work or not. In this chapter, we shall not cover the zoning requirements and the process thereof as the subject is a book on its own. However, once the Town Planner has compiled and concluded the report and your site meets the requirement, he submits it to your local municipality/ authority for approval (note that this process can take some months to be approved depending on the effectiveness and efficiencies of the process of an individual municipality).

Step 2:   *Land Survey:* Once the Town Planner has confirmed that the site does meet the requirements for the subdivision process, you will then have to appoint a Land Surveyor. Land Surveyor will then conduct the land survey to demarcate the boundaries for each site in accordance with the Town Planner's recommendations, produce site plans, and report which will form part of the Town Planner's application to the municipality.

Step 3: *Approval of site plans:* After the Town Planner has submitted the plans and application to the municipality and they are approved, you can now communicate with the municipality for the installation of underground services. Once the underground services have been installed, you may start with the construction of roads if applicable.

Step 4: *Selling of sites*: Once all the services have been installed and roads are constructed and approved, you can now start the process of appointing an estate agent (now known as property practitioner) to list the sites for sale and sell them and make money.

Chapter 25: Land Consolidation

There are times whereby you will have a site that is too small to fit your structural property plan or find two sites that are adjacent to each but still don't meet your site plan requirements. For example, you want a structure or building that will cover the surface area of 6000m2 but your current site can only accommodate 4000m2, the site adjacent to yours is on sale, and it can cover a surface area of 3500m2. You will have to make sure that you purchase this site so that you can be able to meet your goals of building a 6000m2 structure of a building.

Therefore, in a nutshell, Land Sub-division is a strategy that involves the purchase of one or more sites to combine them to be one big site land. The process includes the appointment of town planner, land surveyor, and approval of site plans together with the application of site consolidation from the local municipality or authority.

Chapter 26: Rent-To-Own

A healthy credit score is critical whenever you want to buy properties using a bond from the bank. To qualify for a bond, potential buyers usually need to have saved enough to put down a deposit, or if you are a first-time buyer, you might qualify for a 100% bond. Therefore, it is very important to start by consulting the bond originator so that you may understand whether do you qualify for a bond or not. What if not? Don't worry about that, as a property investor, there are other alternatives that you may explore, and one of them will be discussed in this chapter which is a rent-to-own strategy.

The rent-to-own strategy is whereby a property investor enters into a lease arrangement that provides for the rental of a property for an agreed period. At the end of it, the investor has the option to buy. This applies especially to the investors who are unable to qualify for a bond traditionally. Rent-to-own provides a window of time in which to build up both a deposit and a healthy credit history.

What's interesting with a rent to own strategy is that it gives you the freedom to back out of the deal whenever you want, and it won't affect your credit rating at all. This is possible because you will be treated as if you were involved in a normal lease agreement.

How to find these deals? First of all, look out for property developers' websites that sell properties and deals like these. Secondly, look out for properties that are listed or advertised by the owners, not the property practitioners. Normally, and in most cases, when a property is being advertised by the owner, it means that the property is paid off. Therefore, if you find a property that is paid off, it increases your advantage of negotiating for a better deal. Once you have found a property like this, you need to follow a process of buying a house that has been elaborated in many chapters in this book depending on your investment goals.

Chapter 27: Rent-To-Rent

People come from different backgrounds and find themselves in a situation whereby it's difficult to purchase a property. As a property investor, you need to be smart and make money even though you do not own any property as long as you are able to meet the rental requirements.

To achieve this, you need to lease a house, not to rent it out. This means that you must negotiate with the owner of the property to manage the property outright by being responsible for the maintenance, rates and taxes, water, electricity, insurance, and repairs of this property (you indirectly own the house).

Once you have agreed with the owner and have signed the lease agreement, you may now optimally utilize this property to generate revenue because there would be no conditions as to how you can use it. This means that you may apply the multi-let strategy whereby you will own one room, and you rent out other rooms to other tenants and share the living room, kitchen, and bathroom. In this situation, you might be sharing the costs to cover for the lease agreement, and if you have negotiated a good deal with the owner, you might make a profit.

Therefore, it is critical that you choose a good location, which is close to public transport, industries, higher education institutions, or malls. This would assist in finding tenants that require an accommodation that is close to their places of work or study, which would become a high demand for the tenants and rental income. Make sure that you do proper research about the area and do proper calculations. Be willing to cohabit with other people and establish strict but reasonable rules. Whatever profit you make out of this deal, make sure that you save money so that you will be able to buy your property but continue with the same deals.

Closing

Congratulations on making a wise decision to purchase this book and reading through until this point. You have made a huge investment while saved significantly on this book because the information contained in this book would have cost ten thousand rands on our face-to-face mentorship program. Therefore, don't look back, press on, think big, think wealth, think property, and prosper in your financial freedom goals. No one can do it but yourself, please start implementing what you have learned from this book and transfer this knowledge to those that are close to you and your generations to come. Remember that speed kills, therefore take one step at the time, start by crawling, then walk before you can run so that achieve your goals accordingly.

You have now learned how to start investing in the residential property business, what is important going forward is to find a Mentor (not just any mentor but property investment mentor) who will guide you over and above what you have learned in this book. Be specific on your goals and make sure that you work on your business and not in it by making sure that you select a great and productive mastermind team that will assist you to achieve your goals. Don't stop learning, continue to attend property investment seminars, watch property investment videos on my YouTube channel, and please subscribe and like it, to access it, type Mpho Hadebe on YouTube.

One important thing that you shouldn't forget is that, in the property business, you make money when you buy and not when you sell, therefore you must make sure that the property that you are buying meets the following two criteria: the property must have equity and either the property or the seller must be destressed. If it doesn't meet these two criteria, please walk away because you will not make any profit out of that property just like the ordinary investors.

Please if you find this book useful and informative, go to Amazon and post your positive reviews and like the book so that it can be seen by other people and become the number one bestseller book. And if you need more information on our mentorship program please don't hesitate to inbox Mpho Hadebe on Facebook

About the Author

Mpho Hadebe is a Mentor, Entrepreneur, Founder, and Managing Director for Ellion Property Solutions, specializing in property investment training and mentorship, based in South Africa. He holds Btech Degree in Civil Engineering from the Durban University of Technology in South Africa and a Master's Degree in Logistics and Supply Chain at the Netherland Maritime University in Rotterdam.

Mr. Hadebe has accumulated a lot of experience from managing ports and rail infrastructure, roads, and building projects. He started investing in property from 2007 and since then he has gained more interest and knowledge on investing in property. Mpho has trained more than 1000 property investors around South Africa and mentored more than 30 property investment mentees.

www.ingramcontent.com/pod-product-compliance
Lightning Source LLC
Chambersburg PA
CBHW040231220526
45473CB00001B/203